SPALD
BOXING

Are used by the Champions of the World.

Above illustrates the patent palm lacing and patent palm grip referred to in descriptions of following boxing gloves. With these improvements we believe our line is absolutely the finest on the market. The patent palm lacing insuring a snug fit at all times is a very valuable feature, and the patent palm grip we know will be appreciated by those who want gloves that are up-to-date in every particular.

No. **11. Corbett pattern, large 7 oz. glove,** gambia tan leather, padded with best curled hair, patent palm lacing, padded wristband, patent palm grip. Substantially made throughout for hard usage. Per set, **15/-**

No. **9. Regulation 5 oz. glove,** otherwise same as No. 11. Per set, **15/-**

No. **13. Corbett pattern,** olive tanned leather, well padded with hair, patent palm lacing and patent palm grip. Per set, **12/6**

No. **14. Regulation 5 oz. glove,** dark wine colour, padded wristband, patent palm lacing and palm grip. Per set, **11/6**

No. **15. Corbett pattern,** soft tanned leather, well padded with hair, padded wristband, patent palm lacing and patent palm grip. Per set, **10/6**

No. **23. Regular pattern,** outer handpiece of olive tanned leather, grip and cuffs of darker shade, hair padded and patent palm lacing. Per set, **5/6**

Our Illustrated Art Catalogue (No. 56) on Boxing Goods sent free upon application. Please mention "Boxing."

A. G. SPALDING & BROS.

ATHLETIC GOODS MANUFACTURERS

53, 54 & 55 FETTER LANE, LONDON, E.C.

Boxing

ATTITUDE: AFTER SHAKING HANDS. (See p. 21.)

BOXING

WITH A SECTION ON SINGLE-STICK

By

A. J. Newton

Light-Weight Amateur Champion 1888 and 1890

BLOOMSBURY

First published 1910 under the title *Boxing, with a Section on Single-stick* by C. Arthur Pearson Limited

This edition published by Bloomsbury Publishing in 2005

The moral right of the author has been asserted

Bloomsbury Publishing Plc, 36 Soho Square, London W1D 3QY

A CIP catalogue record for this book is available from the British Library

ISBN 0 7475 7906 7
ISBN-13 780747579069

10 9 8 7 6 5 4 3 2 1

Printed by Clays Ltd, St Ives plc

All papers used by Bloomsbury Publishing are natural, recyclable products
made from wood grown in well-managed forests. The manufacturing
processes conform to the environmental regulations of the country of origin.

http://www.bloomsbury.com

It is advisable to check with your doctor before embarking on any exercise
programme. A physician should be consulted in all matters relating to health.
Neither the author nor the publisher can accept legal responsibility
for any injury sustained while following the exercises

Contents

Contents

Contents

Contents

Boxing

INTRODUCTION

As an expert boxer, and an established master of the art who has taught many champions, professional and amateur, on lines which have led to their success, I may claim the right to speak with some authority upon the practical and scientific methods and advantages of boxing.

It is true that the most elaborate instructions, given in the best of books, can never take the place of actual practice in the ring, but the advice and indirect guidance of any recognised expert is always helpful, and an up-to-date text book will convey many useful hints and lessons, which supplement and confirm the necessary personal work and training of the pugilist.

I trust therefore that these pages will set many a beginner on the right course, and add some fresh points of value to the experience of those who are already skilled in the use of the gloves.

CHAPTER I

The Value of Boxing

Self-defence a natural instinct—A healthy sport—A moral discipline—School boxing—Adult boxing.

Self-defence a Natural Instinct.

THE idea of self-defence is natural to most men. As a race, the British in particular have bred into the very bone of them independent, and hence on occasion pugilistic, determination. To them self-defence instinctively implies a use of the fists—boxing. A native of southern Europe in excitement or dispute flies to his knife or dagger. The wild westerner grips his six-shooter, but the Britisher, wherever you may find him, is handy with his fists in an emergency.

This is an undoubted fact, but how very few of us know how to make the most effective and scientific use of our natural means of attack or defence.

In this little work I shall endeavour to lay before the reader all the necessary strokes, lunges, parries, feints, attacks, or retirements which are the necessary equipment of a first-rate boxer.

School Boxing

A Healthy Sport.

Boxing is a thoroughly healthy sport, and of ideal value for development of sound wind and fine free lung action, for it exercises every muscle of the body from the toes to the finger-tips. The taking and giving of blows create muscle of the best sort, such as can instantly be as soft as jelly or as hard as iron at will.

In these ways it equals rowing, and is superior to any other form of exercise.

A Moral Discipline.

There is no finer course of moral discipline, nor is there any better temper-sweetener than a training with "the mittens." The most irascible boy or man will be improved if he goes in for boxing. Bad temper cannot live through it, for it not only does not pay but absolutely becomes a disadvantage to its owner.

There is nothing which encourages cool, calm judgment, combined with quick decision, so thoroughly as boxing.

School Boxing.

Many a boy has been turned from a spoilt and pampered pet into a manly boy of generous but firm character in the gymnasium boxing-class at his school. The fond mother who, attending a school tournament, sees the ruby flow from her son's nose as the result of a smart tap from the glove of a quicker youngster is apt to form an unfavourable opinion of the art, but

Adult Boxing

nevertheless it is, under proper rules and supervision, quite a harmless recreation and one which carries abundant benefits in its train.

Adult Boxing.

"Boxing is a dangerous sport, and I cannot afford to take any risks. I work for my living, and have others dependent upon me, so I cannot go in for it." In imagination I hear this said by many a busy man.

But is boxing dangerous? I answer emphatically, "No." Contest for contest there are fewer accidents or injuries at boxing, even including endurance contests (fights to a finish), than at most other games. Now and again a man with a weak heart enters on a severe endurance contest with fatal results, but in every case which is thoroughly well investigated, the unhappy result proves to have come about in consequence of the boxer's permanent weakness, and not directly from the boxing.

With this short preliminary flourish in favour of the art which I profess and teach, I now proceed to initiate the inexperienced into the mysteries of "leads," "cross counters," "slips," and the thousand and one points which conduce to the equipment of an amateur or champion boxer.

CHAPTER II

Positions in Boxing

Variety useful—Points of importance—Experts' opinions—
The correct attitude—Incorrect attitudes—Correct hand
action—Incorrect hand action—Correct leg action—Body
movements.

No two boxers, or writers on boxing, are quite agreed
on the subject of the best position to adopt. Nearly
every champion boxer or fighter has a style of standing "on guard," which is in some respect his own.

Variety Useful.

Every boxer should be quite at home in several
positions, and whilst he will of course soon discover
a favourite attitude, he should in the course of a bout
change this just as he varies his attack. It all helps
to disconcert the opponent and upset his plans based
on the first attitude, if on meeting, say for other
rounds, he finds your attitude and method of attack
altered from that of the first.

Points of Importance.

The points to be considered are :—

(1) To present the least possible vulnerable space
toward your opponent.

Points of Importance

(2) So to stand as to be possessed of the utmost power of movement in any direction, for the purpose of attack or retirement.

(3) To have a firm position to resist attack without loss of balance or mobility.

As to the first point almost every one agrees that the best angle of the body is that of the dotted line (Fig. 1). It is usual to stand thus with the

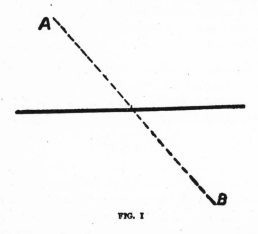

FIG. 1

left shoulder forward, but there are men who find they fight better with the right forward, in which case the angle would be the same, but reversed as in Fig. 2.

In either event, the shoulder which is forward is held a little higher than the other, and so forms a protection for the chin, which, as will be seen later, is the most vulnerable part.

18

Experts' Opinions

It is on points Nos. 2 and 3 that the most differences of opinion exist, so I give my readers the varied views of several experts.

Experts' Opinions.

Captain W. Edgworth-Johnstone, the best of all army boxers, and amateur champion of Great Britain

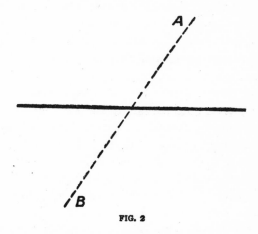

FIG. 2

in 1895 and 1896, holds that[1] the distance between the feet should be about $2\frac{1}{4}$ times the length of the foot.

Weight fairly evenly distributed on either leg, with a shade more on the rear leg, and borne principally on the front half of the feet. Legs slightly bent.

[1] " Boxing " (Gale & Polden), page 8.

Experts' Opinions

R. G. Allanson-Winn[1] considers that for a 5 ft. 10 in. man, who stands left foot forward, the right foot should be 15 to 18 ins. behind the left, and inclined to the line on which that foot is, at an angle of 30° to 45°, and about 6 or 8 ins. to the right of that line. Left foot in a straight line pointing to adversary's face. Legs not to be bent at all. He is most emphatic on this point.

Weight to be absolutely equally balanced on both legs; for he adds: "If you are not thus evenly poised, and have, say, half as much weight again on your right leg as you have on the left, you will, if you want to advance, have all the effort of shifting three-quarters of your weight suddenly instead of only half."

Ned Donelly, formerly a prize-fighter and afterwards boxing instructor, says: "Distance between feet for 5 ft. 8 in. man should be 14 ins. Rear foot directly behind front foot and turned slightly outwards, with its heel raised about 2 ins. from the ground. Left foot flat, knees slightly bent."

Robert Fitzsimmons believes in slightly bent legs. Weight of body carried on right foot. To find correct distance for feet, he recommends standing near a wall poised as above. The left fist stretched forward with arm bent a little at the elbow, so that the knuckles touch the wall. Now, if a hard push throws you out of position, the feet are too close together.

[1] "Boxing" (All England Series), page 5.   Bell & Son.

The Correct Attitude

The Correct Attitude.

All of these positions have points in their favour, and should be practised; but as a standard correct position, I recommend the following :—

Feet about 1½-foot's length apart. Front foot pointing straight towards opponent. Heel of rear foot about 3 inches to the side of the line of front foot. Rear foot at angle of 45° from line of front foot. Weight rather more on rear foot than on front, and borne on the front part of each foot. Legs very slightly bent, just sufficient to allow of instantaneous movement, without the necessity of a further bend to start the movement.

The arm which is forward should be held slightly bent at the elbow, with the thumb of the hand uppermost, so keeping the back of the hand vertical from the ground. The height at which the hand is held must necessarily vary according to the height of the opponent—higher for a taller, and lower for a shorter adversary. The average height should be on a horizontal line with the forward nipple of the chest.

The rear or "guard" arm should lie across the chest—the elbow well in to side, the back of the hand uppermost. The fingers of the clenched hand, and the inner side of forearm should actually touch the body. The elbow of this arm will lie just above the belt, and the hand against the forward nipple.

Correct Hand Action

Incorrect Attitudes.

Perhaps the commonest of faults of attitude amongst amateurs are connected with the arms and hands.

The forward arm is stretched stiffly straight forward.

The backs of the hands are held downwards. This is a very common mistake, though why it is adopted I cannot conceive, seeing that it entails a distinct effort to turn the backs of the hands downwards, and puts the muscles of the arms into an unnatural, tiring, and strained position between the hits, when they should be in comparative repose.

The legs are straddled too widely apart.

The toe of the front foot is turned inwards, and the rear foot is held directly behind the front foot, leaving the boxer in a most convenient position for his opponent to upset his equilibrium.

The legs are held quite straight and stiff. In walking when in this position the legs are termed "locked," which name in itself suggests how inappropriate such a position must be to a boxer who requires constant spring and agility, not a fixed position.

Correct Hand Action.

The hands should be held loosely closed between hits, and only be clenched at the instant of landing or guarding a blow. It is a great and unnecessary strain to keep them tightly closed all the time.

Incorrect Hand Action

The left hand should be kept constantly moving. This is less tiring than holding it stationary.

Even more important is the fact that whilst on the move a hit can be delivered with less notice to the opponent than from a still arm, for if a still arm and hand are moved the opponent sees it instantly; but if a moving arm and hand deliver a blow it is well on its way before the opponent notices that it is anything other than its ordinary feint; provided that the blow is delivered without any obvious withdrawal of the arm.

The left hand should take a backward and forward movement over a space of about six or eight inches. It should not move on a level, but in a sort of segment of a circle.

The right hand may also move a few inches backwards and forwards, which means that it will travel from just before the left nipple to just beyond it and back again.

Incorrect Hand Action.

Keeping the hands dead still until a blow is struck.

Turning the hands round from the wrists and elbows. This is wrong, because during such turns they are not ready to strike without the turn being completed, or a reverse movement made to bring hand, wrist, and arm into one straight instrument for the blow.

Sawing the right forearm and elbow too far away from the body.

Correct Leg Action.

All the best boxing instructors are agreed that the novice must study leg action before anything else.

Correct Leg Action

The finest knowledge of blows and how to deliver them is absolutely useless, unless the boxer knows how to use his legs. The strongest and heaviest man can be knocked clean off his legs by a small skilful opponent if he does not know how to stand and move. I consider a man who is learning boxing should not face an opponent even for a practice spar until he has had several lessons in leg action.

There are several general rules, of which the following are the chief.

Advancing, the foremost leg takes the lead, followed by the near leg, which comes forward just so far as to leave it the same distance behind the front one before.

In retiring the rear leg moves first, and is followed by the front leg.

If the wrong leg is moved first either in advancing or retiring momentary loss of stability ensues, during which a light touch from opponent will bring about a knock down.

Never work round the right of an opponent, always keep moving to the left. There are occasions when one is compelled by the adversary to break ground to the right, but this should never be done of one's own choice. In moving to the right when compelled to do so the right foot moves first.

The novice should practice jumping backwards and forwards without the relative positions of the feet being altered. A clear spring backwards will sometimes be most opportune, but in boxing it is not well to make a habit of this, for it necessitates both feet being off the ground at once, in which position a comparatively light

Body Movements

touch from the antagonist will prove a knock-down blow.

Some of the very best boxers keep the feet always moving between hits, just as the hands are never allowed to be still. Bob Fitzsimmons in all his big fights has kept his feet on the move in what has aptly been described as "an ungainly shuffle," but it has contributed not a little to his frequent successes.

In moving to the left the rear foot goes first, and is followed by the front foot. When breaking to the right the front foot moves first and the rear foot follows. In both these cases a step of about a foot at a time is as long as is desirable, and the distance between the feet should be maintained.

Body Movements.

The body itself should also be kept moving, apart from its being carried about by the legs. A slight backwards and forwards swaying or swinging motion of the trunk from the hips is good. It conduces to a general readiness of the body to spring to any position it may be called upon to occupy, such as a quick draw-back or bend-back, or forwards or sideways.

CHAPTER III

Leading

Definition of Leading.

LEADING is practically the assumption of the attack, as distinguished from striking blows in return for or to forestall those of one's opponent. The recognised leads, which are five in number, may be described as—

      (1) Left hand lead at head.
      (2) Left hand lead at body.
      (3) Right hand lead at head.
      (4) Right hand lead at body.
      (5) Double leads.

The Left Hand Lead at Head.

This is the lead most frequently used in boxing. By its means more fights have been won than can be credited to any other blow. This preference and success is probably due to the fact that, owing to the attitude of boxers, the left hand driven straight at the head of one's adver-

Faults to be Avoided

sary has less distance to travel than in any other hit. It is also admirably adapted for adding the whole weight of the body and a push from the right leg to its force.

This then is the first stroke which the novice should practice, and if he learns to deliver it quickly, straight, and with his weight behind it, no amount of practice need be considered too great for the result achieved.

Faults to be Avoided.

The commonest faults are :—

Hitting from above downwards like a hammer stroke. A blow should be delivered quite straight, or in a slightly upward plane if the opponent is the taller man.

Striking every time alike, that is with the head in the same position. The head should be sometimes held high, sometimes low, and sometimes with the right hand in front of it as guard.

Overreaching in the endeavour to drive a blow well home. Practice is the only means of learning exactly how far you can land it with advantage. More men are brought down by overreaching themselves than any other fault.

Delivering the blow "round," thereby entailing a longer journey for the fist to its goal.

Hitting with back of hand downwards which deprives the stroke of half its force.

The Correct Method.

If the opponent's guard is a little low, without any warning, whilst the left hand is in the course of its "resting" circular movement before described, advance the left foot and drive out the fist straight for

FOR LEFT HAND LEAD DUCK AND LEFT HAND HALF-ARM
ON CHIN. (See p. 29.)

How to Guard the Left Lead

opponent's head, clench the hand just as it lands. The knuckles of the first and second fingers should be the part of the hand to strike your opponent; this necessitates the back of the hand being rather more up than down, and the palm and fingers inwards. A push from the right leg lends force and finish to the blow.

If one gets well home with a left lead without opponent having got in an exchange hit, one cannot do better than follow it up without altering one's position at all with several more quick hits with the same hand one after the other on opponent's head. These will not be hard hits, but all count as points in a competition, and are confusing to the adversary.

How to Guard the Left Lead.

There is a choice of quite a number of guards to this hit.

(1) Ducking head to right, and allowing opponent to run his ribs on to the point of your left shoulder, or counter with left on chin.

(2) Ducking to left, and delivering right on opponent's ribs.

(3) Ducking to right, and left hand punch in ribs.

(4) Side-stepping or slipping, and knocking opponent's lead aside.

(5) Knocking up opponent's fist and arm with left, and delivering right on "the mark." This is known as "blocking."

(6) Knocking down opponent's lead with left, and landing right on left side of his jaw

LEFT HAND LEAD, DUCK, AND COUNTER WITH RIGHT
ON BODY. (See p. 29.)

Left Hand Lead at Body

(7) Drawing back the head and shoulders far enough to avoid his lead.

(8) Knocking up opponent's fist with right.

(9) Knocking up opponent's fist with left.

(10) Outside Left Counter (see Chapter VI.).

(11) Inside Left Counter (see Chapter VI.).

(12) Side-stepping, allowing opponent's left to pass over your left shoulder, and punching him with right on head or body.

All these methods should be practised, as variety of attack and guard and return go a very long way towards confusing your opponent and taking the confidence out of his attack. Nos. 10 and 11 are perhaps the best and most usual way of meeting a left hand lead. They are described and explained in Chapter VI. on Countering. No. 12 is also very effective; perhaps the body hit in this case is better than the head.

In all forms of withdrawal to avoid attack it should be borne in mind that the less energy expended the better, and if your head is ducked so as to allow opponent's lead to pass not more than half an inch away, it is better than if you avoided it by two inches; for not only is force saved, but your position is less altered.

Save all possible energy for your own attack.

Left Hand Lead at Body.

This is a very effective blow if brought off successfully, but it lays one much more open to punishment, and is more difficult to land home than the lead with the same hand at the head.

GUARD FOR LEFT HAND LEAD AT HEAD. (See p. 3I.)

Defence and Counter

The deliverer must be prepared to spring quickly back, and hence must also see that he has room to do so.

It is best to make a feint at the head to induce opponent to raise his body-guard and allow of your landing on the "mark."

In striking the blow step well in, and duck head to the right, to avoid your opponent's left lead at head, also raise your body guard in readiness to meet a left hand upper cut, should your opponent's whim be in that direction.

A strong body swing is added to the blow, which may be made a complete knock-out if it strikes the mark accurately and hard enough. This swing, however, lends force to the opponent's blow whether it be left lead at the head or upper cut, if one is caught "on the move."

Defence and Counter.

The two blows mentioned above are the most effective stops or counters—

(1) Left hand at head.

(2) A left hand upper cut.

For the first, divining your opponent's intention, you punch him on the head with your left hand before he can get his head down and his blow home. Skilful judgment and timing is necessary for this stop hit.

The second is also a counter hit. Just as your opponent's head comes down, and his hit lands, you simultaneously land in his face with an upper cut from your left. The movement towards you of opponent's head doubles the force of your hit.

Right Hand Lead at Head

Guards to Left Hand Body Blow.

There are two guards to the left hand body blow—

(1) Keeping the rear arm firmly against the body across the mark, so that the blow lands on the guarding forearm.

(2) A step back out of distance.

A man who is taller than his opponent can draw back his body from his opponent's lead, and, leaning forward his own left shoulder, can land his left on opponent's face, or his right as in p. 44.

Right Hand Lead at Head.

This is not nearly so safe a hit as its left hand equivalent, but it can nevertheless sometimes be dealt with considerable success. It must be preceded by a feint—preferably the left at the body—followed immediately by the right on to the chin.

It is necessary to step well in towards the adversary, and the blow must be dealt more rapidly than perhaps almost any other, for the right hand has so far to go to reach its mark that opponent has more time to formulate and execute his defence, or stop, or counter, than in the case of other hits.

An excellent plan after the feint is to place the left over, and to so occupy opponent's left, at the instant of sending home the right.

In leading with the right hand at head it is usually advisable to duck your head somewhat to the left, as this helps to avoid counter hit from opponent's right or left.

34

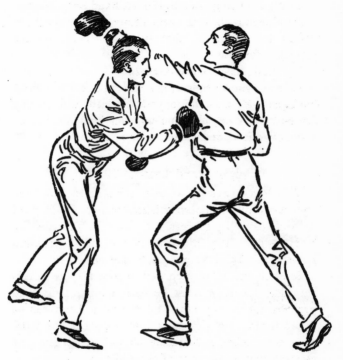

THE SIDE-STEP AND RIGHT COUNTER ON THE BODY. (See p. 31.)

Right Hand Lead at Body

The moment you see the opening for a right lead the right foot must be advanced a trifle so as to square the body. The best opening to look for is when opponent appears about to swing his left at your body.

Defence and Counter to Right at Head.

There is no really good guard for this hit, but plenty of opening for anticipation or retaliation. Some recommend as a guard the receiving the blow on the left elbow or forearm, but I do not advise this. The blow may be dodged or turned by an outward stroke of the left, but the best thing to do is to hit out straight with the left at opponent's chin. Your left hand has considerably less distance to travel than opponent's right, and if you succeed in anticipating his blow, he receives the benefit of his own forward movement, added to your onset.

Right Hand Lead at Body.

This is not a knock-out blow, but if landed several times on the same spot, becomes very aggravating and trying to the receiver.

The best method of delivery is to step well in with the forward foot, feint with the left at head and with the left strike aside opponent's left. Swing the body round from right to left and land the punch on left side of adversary's ribs.

Ned Donelly, in his excellent little volume "Self-Defence" (Wyman & Son, Ltd.), recommends landing on the mark, but this is much more difficult to achieve, as opponent's guard hand must also be persuaded to leave its position while the left hand is being diverted.

Double Leads

Defence of Right Lead at Body.

It may be guarded (1) by the guard arm; (2) the left arm may be lowered against the body and receive the blow. In this case there is an opening to get in a right swing on opponent's face before he can get away again.

If the left hand has not been knocked aside, a straight left, just as in the case of the left lead at body, may be landed before opponent can get home.

Double Leads.

There are quite a number of double leads, of which the following are the principal :—

(1) The left at body and head.
(2) The left at body, right at head.
(3) The left at head, right at body.
(4) Both hands at body.
(5) Both hands at head.

Double leads are not, as might be supposed, two simultaneous punches, but are two punches delivered one after the other, as rapidly as possible; in fact I would describe them as a postman's knock, a rat-tat.

Modern American fighting has developed the double lead considerably; in fact the policy of very many transatlantic boxers is to execute a series of rushes and double leads, followed by a clinch or a spring back retirement out of distance.

As a general rule double leads with the left hand are more successful than those in which the right takes part.

FOR LEFT HAND LEAD STEP OUTSIDE AND COUNTER ON BODY
WITH THE LEFT. (See p. 31.)

CHAPTER IV

The Guard

*Definition of the guard—Its proper value—Circumstances
alter cases—Guarding may be action—The usual guard
—A caution—Double guard—Parrying.*

Definition of the Guard.

THE attitude in which the boxer faces his opponent is
termed " on guard," and the hand (usually the right)
which is kept to the rear, and lies across the chest, is
usually known as the " guard" hand.

As will be gathered in different parts of this treatise,
the " guard" hand is also used for hitting, but, being
a longer distance away from the opponent, it is better
placed than the forward hand for the purpose of
defence. It can quickly reach any position in front of
the head or body to " guard" a coming hit.

It is also well placed for parrying or striking up
and out of its aimed course the opponent's hand as it
approaches to deliver a blow.

Its Proper Value.

Guarding should be regarded as a " fall back upon,"
not as a regular habit. As has been pointed out in
other places, Countering, Ducking, and Withdrawing
are generally better tactics.

By guarding you save yourself a blow and baulk
your opponent a point, but you do not score one, and

Guarding may be Action

you lose the opportunity of turning your opponent's impetus against himself.

Let not the uses of guarding, however, be too much underrated, for there are times when it is invaluable.

Circumstances alter Cases.

When fighting a man of superior strength who comes with a rush that will not be gainsaid, and you are hard pressed, guarding with both hands sometimes becomes not merely the best policy, but the only one.

Guarding may be Action.

Guarding also often forms a part of leading. If your opponent always answers your left lead with a left counter, it will occasionally pay to lead with the left, whilst the right guards the chin, and receives opponent's counter hit.

Guarding assists several other hits which are described in different parts of this volume.

As a general rule guarding is more serviceable where body blows are concerned than for those at the head, which can generally with greater advantage be ducked to one side or the other.

The Usual Guard.

The most usual guard is to leave the rear hand and arm lying across the abdomen, so that the elbow is just above the belt on the right side of the body, and the forearm slopes upward in front of the body covering the "mark" or spot just below the sternum or bone to which the ribs are fastened in front, whilst the fist and glove cover the left chest nipple.

40

GUARD AND COUNTER FOR LEFT HAND BODY LEAD. (See pp. 33-4.)

A Caution

In this position, without any movement at all, the most accessible and vulnerable parts of the body are covered.

A Caution.

Care must be taken that the arm actually lies against the body, touching it, for if it were held loosely away from the flesh of the body the force of blows guarded would be felt almost as severely as if they were not guarded at all. A most important point in guarding is that the back of the hand must be turned quite upwards from the forearm, this gives treble resisting strength.

It is important also that the stomach should be drawn in, and the abdominal muscles contracted at the instant of the guard arm receiving a blow.

Double Guard.

We have already noted that when very hard pressed the double guard *may*, and sometimes *must* be resorted to. The right hand covers the chin and face, and its forearm guards the right side of the ribs and abdomen. The palm of the right glove is held facing opponent. The left arm is lowered so that it protects the left side of body, and its forearm and glove across the left side of abdomen and the "mark."

Parrying.

Parrying, or diverting blows, is a most essential form of guarding, for it throws the opponent off his course, may upset his balance, and often lays him open to receive a very punishing hit instead of dealing one.

CHAPTER V

Ducking and Side-Stepping,
or Slipping

*Value of ducking—Do not overdo it—Playing to the gallery
—The right sort of ducking—The side-step, or slip.*

As ducking and side-stepping, or slipping, are an
absolute avoidance of hits, rather than the receiving
but guarding them, they are here considered in a
short chapter by themselves.

Value of Ducking.

Ducking is the most frequently used move on the
boxer's board.   There is no better method of avoiding
a hit, for ducking in nearly every case puts the
ducker in a position to hit a blow, as well as to
avoid one.

In the description of many leads and counters, it
will be noticed that a duck of the head either to
right or left is included.

Do not Overdo It.

To the alert active small man ducking becomes
very fascinating; in fact after a time his care must
be not to overdo it. It is a very effective dodge

RIGHT HAND STOP FOR SWINGING LEFT AT BODY OR HEAD.
(See p. 34.)

The Right Sort of Ducking

so far as the onlookers are concerned, and a clever escape from punishment by ducking will nearly always evoke applause or congratulatory comment from spectators of a bout. This tends to make the man who is a little proud of himself, and keen for applause, resort to this move too frequently. Some very skilful boxers have spoiled themselves by over-indulgence in what may be termed "show off" ducking.

Playing to the Gallery.

Pedlar Palmer was perhaps the cleverest ducker I have ever seen, but he always seemed even in his serious encounters to be trying to win applause rather than to use this dodge solely for practical purposes of defence. In his fight with the American feather-weight champion, Terry M'Govern, it proved his undoing, for the little American had prepared for this, and steering Palmer's head with his left hand at the last of two or three successive ducks, into position, he knocked him clean out with the right, and in the first round too. One of my cleverest bantam pupils, Tom Rippington, became a victim on one occasion through gallery play of a similar nature.

The Right Sort of Ducking.

The best plan is to make it a fixed rule never to duck without at the same time striking a blow.

Don't duck too deeply. Some men swing their heads round and round as though they were attached to their bodies by a little piece of string.

The Side-Step, or Slip

Always bear in mind that your object is *just to miss* the blow, and to do so with the least possible effort, or movement from your fighting attitude. At the same time discretion must play a part, as there is such a thing as cutting it too fine, and being caught.

The body is in some cases slightly lowered as the head is bent to one side, but only in case of necessity, or when accompanying a duck forward with a step in and a low body blow.

The Side-Step, or Slip.

The side-step is a combination of the ducking movement with a step forward. The method of its successful accomplishment is as follows.

Meet the left-hand blow of your opponent aimed at your head by ducking to the right completely under his arm, at the same time stepping past him with the left foot in such a way that your body almost grazes his. Immediately bring your right foot up to a position some twelve inches in advance of your left, delivering as your adversary lunges past you a heavy blow on the left side of his chin. You must be very careful not to let your hit land on the back of his neck, as such a blow would be instantly proclaimed a foul. (See p. 35.)

This piece of strategy is extremely useful in tight corners, or when driven against the ropes. It is often possible to escape from what appears to be a desperate predicament by unexpectedly resorting to it.

DRAW AND COUNTER WITH RIGHT ON·THE POINT OR THROAT
AS ILLUSTRATED. (See p. 34.)

CHAPTER VI

The Counter, Time Hit, or Stop

Uses of the counter—Personal error is a factor—Particular points—General maxims—Left head counter—Left body counter—Right head counter—Right body counter—Left cross counter—Right cross counter.

Uses of the Counter.

IN the Badminton volume which treats of the art of boxing—the first and foremost description, before attacking or leads are dealt with at all—comes the "stop" by countering.

It is pointed out that "boxing" is always known as "self-defence," and hence the very best defensive action which also at one and the same time serves the purpose of inflicting punishment upon the adversary should be mastered first.

It is true that in most cases time hitting, stopping, or countering, call it which you will, for the three terms are synonymous, is the most important method of defence, but it by no means follows that it should be the first thing learnt. So much judgment, delicate timing and absolute accuracy of action are required in this branch of the art, that I consider it should be left by the novice or rather his teacher until

48

one of the later lessons. Many a man has been brought down by a really inferior opponent by relying too confidently on his countering.

Counter-hitting consists of divining at its inception the direction of your opponent's lead, and thwarting it by means of a hit of your own which lands first, and either prevents his blow from reaching its destination, or at any rate robs it of three parts of its sting.

Some men never learn to counter to advantage. A man may be a fine fast and firm hitter, a good guarder and a clever dodger, and yet never become a clever counterer.

The element of what is known to scientists as "personal error" plays a great part in this defence. This is made up of several parts. First, discovering opponent's intention, next, deciding which counter hit shall be given, and then executing the hit decided upon.

All these must be accomplished in the fraction of a second during which opponent's hand travels say a couple of feet, and yet the blow must land before his!

Personal Error is a Factor.

Roughly described, "personal error" is the time which elapses between the mind deciding on an action and the body getting to work to execute it. This varies in different cases. The telegraphic system from brain to muscles works more rapidly in some people than others.

49   D

GUARD FOR RIGHT HAND LEAD AT HEAD. (See p. 36.)

General Maxims

Those in whom it works most speedily will, other points being equal, prove the best counterers.

Particular Points.

The questions of height, reach, length of arm, &c., also enter. The taller of two men will have the advantage over the shorter in the matter of "stopping hits," seeing that his forward arm has less distance to travel to reach his shorter opponent, whilst the latter has also less distance to travel *in the course of his own hit* to receive the counter.

General Maxims.

The following may be taken as general maxims as to countering :—

(1) If you are quicker and taller than your opponent, counter freely whenever an opportunity offers.

(2) If you are quicker and equal in height, counter just as frequently, but have a care that your guard is also up.

(3) If equal both in speed and height, use the counter sparingly; rather resort to ducking, dodging, and side-stepping, just occasionally countering with the view to a surprise successful landing.

(4) If you are inferior in speed and height, play a retiring game, try to draw your opponent to leave you an opening to spring in and do execution, but don't try to counter his blows. It will not come off.

Practice, after the other rudiments of boxing have been acquired, will do much to increase speed

Left Head Counter

Always spar with a quicker man if possible. Nothing beats having to face "example" in this matter. Judgment too, and knack of just getting in to time, can also be more or less learnt.

In favour of the counter let it never be overlooked that one counter successfully steered home is worth two leads duly landed, for the stop-hit has your own punching force and that of your opponent's hit added to it and applied to himself in one dose.

In judging competitions the rule is that, other points being equal, the preference is given to the man who does most leading. Now successful countering has all the appearance to the onlooker of leading, whilst having the tactical advantage of really being and acting on the defensive will count to the boxer, so far as points go, as attacking, an important double advantage.

The recognised counters are :—

       (1) Left Head Counter.
       (2) Left Body Counter.
       (3) Right Head Counter.
       (4) Right Body Counter
       (5) Left Cross Counter.
       (6) Right Cross Counter.

Left Head Counter.

This may be delivered either as an outside or inside counter. The outside is when your left hand and arm travel to the right or outside of opponent's leading arm, and the inside when to the left or inside.

GUARD FOR RIGHT HAND BODY. (See p. 34.)

Left Body Counter

The form your counter takes is according to the blow which it is anticipating.

If opponent leads with his left at head, you dart out your left at his chin, at the same time raising your right to guard your face from his blow; or, instead of using the right to guard, you may duck your head to the right so as to allow his blow to pass over your left shoulder.

It often happens that both men duck to the right, and so each man's fist passes over the other's left shoulder; or each may land their blow on the other's head, so making a left cross counter.

The left counter to a left lead at body by adversary may take two forms, either straight left hand at head, or a left upper cut. These are both described in the chapter on Leading, under the heading of "Defence and Counter to Left Body Blow" (p. 34). The straight hit is the better of the two, as the hand has so short a distance to travel, and hence is more sure of being first in.

The left counter to opponent's right hand lead at head is a straight left hit at the side of point of chin, with one's head ducked to the right to avoid his blow.

Left Body Counter.

This is resorted to when your opponent leads his left at your head. You must step quickly in, and duck to the right, at the same time aiming your left for the "mark." It forms a most effective punch, but the

Left Cross Counter

deliverer must be ready to spring well away instantly after its landing.

Right Head Counter.

This occurs generally as a stop for opponent when he leads right at head. The best plan is to duck your head slightly to the left, to allow his blow to pass over your right shoulder whilst yours hits his chin. It often happens that both bend their heads to left and both blows pass over the shoulders.

A right counter at head is sometimes tried to opponent's left lead at head, but this is a dangerous experiment, as your hand has twice as far as his to travel. Its only real hope of success is when opposed to a left swing hit or a man hitting out of his distance.

Right Body Counter.

This is the body blow described in the chapter on Leading as "Right Hand Lead at Body." In delivering it to counter a left lead at head, duck head well to the left, and strike either for the bottom ribs or the mark.

Left Cross Counter.

This is a "hook" hit, so called because the elbow of the hitting arm (in this case the left) is raised level with the shoulder and fist, forming the arm into a hook; the fist and arm are then swung round to reach the right side of opponent's head. It is delivered against opponent's left lead at head.

55

DOUBLE GUARD WHEN CORNERED. (See p. 42.)

Right Cross Counter

Opinions differ as to the value of this stroke. Some men consider it a most useful one. Others—and I incline to this view—avoid hook hits on account of the liability to injure the hitting arm by a strain or possibly a fracture. On the other hand a left hook has many a time proved a "knock-out."

Right Cross Counter.

The last, but by far the most important of all counters—in fact it may be said to be the most important of all hits in boxing—is the Right Cross Counter.

As your adversary starts his left-hand lead at your head, you step well in, ducking to the left to allow his blow to pass over your right shoulder, and shoot your right straight in from the outside over the shoulder end of his left arm, so as to catch him near the point of the chin.

Swing the right side of your body forward with fullest force, and this together with his impetus makes the hardest of all blows which it is possible to deliver. If the left hand is drawn back it can come quickly in on the right side or jaw, and finish off the work of the right hand.

The back of the hand must be uppermost in this counter, and the blow must always be delivered straight.

CHAPTER VII

The Knock-Out Blow

These are not dangerous—The chin knock-out—An expert's description—The solar plexus blow—Its demoralising effect.

These are not Dangerous.

THE "knock-out" has an awe-inspiring sound, if not even a repulsive one; and yet it is not so dreadful in practice, and carries no ill after effects.

There are two blows, each of which is known as the "knock-out." Either of these punches separately will, if correctly delivered and with due force, be sufficient to send an opponent down and keep him in a state of collapse and unable to rise during the ten seconds limit; but some boxers, and notably Robert Fitzsimmons, who is generally conceded to be the best prize-fighter who ever entered a ring, use the two in conjunction. In such a case the body blow comes first, and is followed up with the chin blow delivered by the same hand.

The Chin Knock-Out.

The most usual and older hit is a hard blow delivered with the full force of the arm and all

58

LEFT HAND LEAD DUCK AND COUNTER WITH THE LEFT ON
THE BODY. (See p. 54.)

An Expert's Description

possible weight and swing of the body, which is landed just a trifle to one side of the chin. If this catches the opponent at a moment when his head and neck are more or less rigid, as they are when he is in the act of "leading," it sets up a pressure on the vertebral arteries, and stops for an instant the blood from flowing up to the brain. The result is that the man falls insensible to the ground. The very act of falling relaxes this compression, and the normal blood flow is soon resumed, so that the man regains consciousness without any bad after effects, other than a slightly dazed feeling for a few minutes.

An Expert's Description.

Perhaps the very best description of the blow which I can give is to quote Captain Edgworth-Johnstone from his most excellent book :—[1]

"The force of the true 'knock-out' depends chiefly upon a swing of the body from the hips, in which the external oblique muscles play a large part; towards the end of the swing, the extensor muscles of the rear leg are sharply braced, pushing the body forward, the swing movement being assisted by jerking back the left arm and shoulder. At the same time, the right shoulder must be shot forward to its fullest extent, and the right arm rapidly extended, with the back of the hand uppermost.

"The effort is a beautifully combined movement, in

1 "Boxing," pp. 140, 141 (Gale & Polden, Amen Corner, E.C.).

The Solar Plexus Blow

which the different muscles successively take their part, the whole weight of the body being thrown in at the moment of impact. On the completion of the blow the right arm, body, and rear leg form a more or less rigid line of resistance.

"The severity of the shock is enormously enhanced should the opponent be caught in a forward movement, in which case his own weight almost doubles its force. The blow must be delivered with lightning-like rapidity and perfect accuracy on the side, but as near the point of the chin as possible, so as to take full advantage of the leverage of the jaw.

"This blow is most commonly brought off, on the opponent's left-hand 'lead' at the face, by means of a right-hand 'cross-counter,' the left side of the chin being found whilst the muscles of the neck and head are in a state of tension from the effort of leading. The consequence is, that the neck experiences a sharp twist, which probably jars the *medulla oblongata* and temporarily compresses the vertebral arteries at the base of the skull, thus checking for an instant the supply of blood to the brain; as a result, the man struck falls down in a dazed condition, and is unable to rise within the mercifully short regulation period of ten seconds."

The Solar Plexus Blow.

The other knock-out hit, which is a later discovery, is known as the Solar Plexus Punch. It is delivered with the left hand on to the opponent's stomach just

DRAW FOR CROSS-COUNTER, DUCK, AND DELIVER STRAIGHT
RIGHT.   (See p. 55.)

The Solar Plexus Blow

below the breastbone, and usually takes the form of a left hook.

Prior to the actual punch the boxer should fight for some time at the head and shoulders of his opponent. This will, after a little while, have the effect of making him pay all his attention to guarding the head and upper part of his body.

All of a sudden a feint is made with the right at the head, up goes the guard, and quick as lightning a step in is taken and the left delivered on the "mark," weight being added by a slight pivot on the foot as the blow lands.

No warning of your intention must be given by look or movement, otherwise the opponent draws back his stomach and involuntarily contracts the oblique, rectal abdominal, and intercostal muscles, protecting the part, and so preventing the jar of the pneumogastric nerve, which is the object of your stroke.

This nerve communicates with the sensitive heart nerves and hinders the heart's action, so stopping it for an instant from pumping blood to the lungs, and causing considerable pain. A spectator receives the impression that the man struck was winded, which, as I have explained, is not really the case.

The man who gives most openings for this hit is he who constantly indulges in right-hand leads as he brings his body square up to the blow, which in this case is delivered with the right hand.

In a competition arranged by the Spartan Harriers,

DRAW AND COUNTER FOR LEFT HAND HOOK, AND DELIVER ON
THROAT OR CHIN. (See p. 55.)

Its Demoralising Effect

I was able to win my heat against W. Dettmer by just such a blow.

Bob Fitzsimmons won nearly all his fights with this blow, instantaneously followed up by the chin-blow delivered with the same hand.

With ordinary boxing gloves it is much more difficult than in a prize-fight to bring off a knock-out with the solar plexus blow.   The size of the glove prevents it sinking into the body far enough to have the desired effect, unless it is most accurately placed and also catches the opponent at a most favourable moment, when his abdomen is well forward and its muscles quite relaxed.

Its Demoralising Effect.

Even though it is not successful with gloves as an actual knock-out, it is a most trying and demoralising hit to one's opponent, and well worth practising.

DRAW AND RIGHT HAND CROSSCOUNTER. (See p. 57.)

CHAPTER VIII

The Clinch

What a clinch is—Scarcely a fair resource—Amateurs and clinching—American prize-fighters' use of it—Barred in boxing.

What a Clinch is.

THE rules of boxing forbid any actual holding, but what is known as the "clinch" comes very near to a hold.

A boxer to avoid punishment steps in right up to his opponent, so that their bodies are as close up to each other as in a wrestle, and he manages, without actually holding, if possible to so entangle his arms with those of the opponent, or round the opponent's body, as to prevent any blow being struck on either side till one of them breaks away.

So clinched, they remain for a few seconds pushing each against the other, and practically wrestling without gripping, on the lookout for an opportunity to break away in the most favourable manner, and to be first in as the attack is renewed.

Scarcely a Fair Resource.

The clinch is an act which, whilst not absolutely disallowed, is very near the border line of a foul.

Barred in Boxing

Amateurs and Clinching.

Amateurs rarely come to a clinch, and if they do, they instantly break loose. If a poll of amateur boxers were taken there is little doubt that this manner would be classed as a foul, and so done away with entirely.

American Prize-fighters.

American prize-fighters indulge in this practice more than any others; in fact it is considered "clever tactics" to fight in a series of "rushes" and "rests," the latter achieved by means of clinching.

Barred in Boxing.

In boxing the referee immediately cautions and separates two competitors who inadvertently (as may sometimes happen) get to a clinch.

CHAPTER IX

Fouls

The breach of any rule is a foul—Accidental fouls—
Intentional fouls—Some common cases.

The Breach of any Rule is a Foul.

ROUGHLY speaking, the contravention of any rule is
a foul—at any rate if it be intentional, or repeated
after a warning has been given by the referee.

Accidental Fouls.

It is possible for a foul to be accidental, and in
such case it is for the referee to decide whether it
is sufficiently serious to give the verdict at once to
the wronged party.

If it is such as would be likely eventually to affect
the result, then, even if palpably accidental, it must
be made to cost the transgressor the bout.

If it be trifling and certainly accidental, the referee
can overlook it.

Intentional Fouls.

If, however, a slight foul action be evidently intentional, the referee must, after a warning, should it
be repeated, give a verdict against the offender.

Some Common Cases

In the case of an intentional and serious foul, the referee must give the match to the wronged party at once.

Some Common Cases.

Hitting with the open hand constitutes a foul blow.

Hitting below the belt is a serious foul.

Tripping constitutes a foul.

Clinching, if repeated after a warning, is sufficient for disqualification. I consider it a cowardly way of avoiding punishment.

Wrestling is a foul action in boxing.

Hitting a man whilst down is fouling.

It is often a matter of difficulty to judge whether hits are fair or foul in the case when one opponent is floored, and the aggressor stands over him to go in and finish the bout as the fallen one rises. The exact instant when a man is "on his feet" or otherwise is difficult to define. It would be well if in every case of a knock-down both men had to retire to their corner for a second or two before recommencing.

In any cases not covered by the rules the referee and the judges together have the power of absolute decision.

CHAPTER X

Miscellaneous Hints

*Sparring and hitting—Advancing—Retiring—Courage
—Keeping cool—The boxer's clothing.*

Sparring and Hitting.

FROM the fact that the National Sporting Club Rules count points, has arisen a style of play that aims not so much at fighting as at mere scoring. This should be discouraged. Boxing has been called the art of self-defence. In a fight with a street rough or a hooligan no one would expect to count points.

Sparring is doubtless very pretty, and invariably draws applause, but preference should always be given to blows that do some business, to good straight hits that do something towards finishing the fight.

A man who has carefully trained himself for brilliant tapping play, will find himself considerably out of it in case he is called upon to do any real work.

Advancing.

Advancing is treated of in the chapter on " Position " earlier in this book.

Courage

Retiring.

Retiring also is considered in the same place.

Courage.

Courage. It is almost laughable to talk of courage in a book on boxing. Courage is taken for granted by every man who stands up between the ropes. And it is well that it should be so. Courage, British bulldog hanging-on pluck wins many a fight against superior odds. Learn to submit yourself to punishment, and you will often be able to weary an opponent who is infinitely stronger than yourself, until the joyous moment when he leaves an opening and you step in to do your share of the fight.

The pluck that helps a man to meet one whom he knows to be a stronger fighter than himself, to meet him and meet him again, round after round, that is the pride of the Boxing Ring and the quality above all others on which rests the reputation of the Briton. In saying this I do not mean to encourage men to take a single blow that they can avoid, I only mean that there must be no element of funk.

Keeping Cool.

Steadiness and self-control are no less important than courage. Once you get flurried or a little out of temper, you give chances innumerable to your wiser and better controlled adversary. The man who keeps cool has half the battle in his hands.

The Boxer's Clothing

The Boxer's Clothing.

For practice, tennis shoes, or even stockings, with a gym shirt, and flannel trousers, make a very useful costume. But for competitions I can do no better than quote the rules laid down on the subject by the Amateur Boxing Association. You must wear "light boots or shoes (without spikes), or socks, with knicker-bockers, breeches, or trousers, and sleeved jerseys."

CHAPTER XI

The Judge and Referee

Duties of the judge—His difficulties—An even balance
—The referee—Distinct from the timekeeper.

Duties of the Judge.

MANY a "first-class fighting man" will tell you that he would any day prefer the place of the beaten man to that of one of the judges. The difficulty of fair judging is enormous, and whatever decision you may finally pronounce in a fairly-won fight, you may be quite sure that someone will quarrel with it. Still somebody must judge, and in case it should fall to your lot to be one of the unfortunates it is just as well to know something about it.

His Difficulties.

The difficulty lies in the almost inevitable bias that intrudes itself on the looker-on at a fight. It is excessively hard to know when you are being fair to one of the two men. You will find yourself unconsciously drawn into partisanship. Also you will often be unable to see for certain what has happened. In such a case do not guess. Your guess is bound to be biassed, if only by the applause of the spectators.

An Even Balance

Try to separate your mind from the body that belongs to it. Perhaps this sounds a little ambiguous. I should say turn yourself into a machine for marking points. You have a piece of paper on which to dot down under the name of each man the points that you consider are his. Every time he lands his fist, dot goes your pencil.

An Even Balance.

At the end of the round you run up the columns, and should the two men appear from your paper to have scored pretty evenly, you must take into account the neatness of the play and the proportion of leading hits.

It may happen that one of the men, being a tricky sparrer, has scored the greater number of points, but has been floored more than once by his less point-seeking opponent. These things must all be taken into consideration.

The Referee.

The business of the referee is to give a casting vote on the not infrequent occasions when the judges disagree, and to superintend the play. If the men seem to him to be very evenly matched and the judges are not unanimous, he may order an extra round, in which case this last round decides the fight without reference to previous fighting.

He must be ever on the watch to warn men whom he detects in foul play, hits with the flat of the hand, &c. And after a couple of warnings he must without

Distinct from the Timekeeper

hesitation disqualify the culprit. The referee has
discretionary powers in cases that cannot be decided
by the rules.

Distinct from the Timekeeper.

The referee has also been expected to keep the
time. But now an independent timekeeper is always
appointed. He has to call "time" at the end of a
round, and to summon the men to the commencement
of the next; and also to count the ten seconds after a
knock-down blow.

CHAPTER XII

Boxing Gloves

Material and price—Approved weight—The best shape.

Material and Price.

IN buying boxing gloves it is advisable to study quality rather than price. The cheapest gloves are covered with chamois leather, but this becomes rough and scratchy, and after a pair have tasted blood, as they are bound to in the course of a career, for a very light tap on the nose or lip in a practice bout will sometimes draw blood, they become hard, and it is positively courting a cut to risk a blow in the face with one of them.

Soft red morocco leather forms the best outer covering. The stuffing should be of the finest quality horsehair.

For the illustrations of boxing gloves and punching balls I am indebted to Frank Bryan, the well-known maker, who supplies the army gymnasia.

Approved Weight.

The Amateur Boxing Association has fixed the minimum weight at 8 oz.

In events at the National Sporting Club taken

part in by professionals, the weight of glove is always specified in the arrangements between the men. As a rule prize-fighters use 6 oz. or 4 oz.

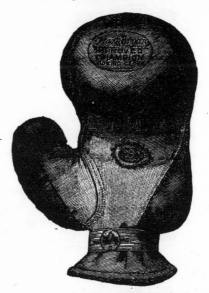

THE ARMY PATTERN GLOVE

gloves. I believe 6 oz. is looked upon as the standard at the above-mentioned club.

The Best Shapes.

There are many varieties of shape. A popular form is that called "The Champion" shown in the above illustration, and this is the army pattern.

I much prefer the new American-shaped glove,

78

The Best Shapes

which has a natural curl in the finger part, and the most decided advantage of the thumb lying

THE AMERICAN-SHAPED GLOVE

behind the hand and finger padding in such style that a sprained thumb is impossible, which cannot be said of any other pattern.

Messrs. Spalding & Bros., of Fetter Lane, E.C., are well known makers of Boxing Gloves, their "Championship" and "Corbett" patterns being highly recommended by some of the best known boxers in the world.

CHAPTER XIII

The Boxer's Wind

Wind of utmost importance—Lung training—Breathing exercises—Quality not quantity—Other breathing exercises—The punching ball—The "Grasshopper"—The army type—The platform—A home-made punching ball—Some hints—The medicine bag—Up stairs and down—Sprinting—Skipping—Jumping—Study variety of exercise.

Wind of Utmost Importance.

IN the ordinary way the care of the "wind" would come in as an item in the chapter on "Training"; but in boxing the possession of a long and strong wind is so essential that I give it a special chapter.

Lung Training.

To be trained "fit" for any branch of athletics implies that the wind is sound, but a man may be quite sound of wind without having had his lungs trained and improved as they might be.

There are many exercises which specially strengthen the chest and breathing apparatus of the body, and I give a few here which every boxer will do well to include in his routine.

Quality not Quantity

Breathing Exercises.

Every morning on getting out of bed, before taking your tub or washing, open the bedroom or bathroom window wide, and standing in front of it expel as much air from your lungs as possible, letting it out through the mouth. When you have breathed out as much as seems possible, draw in the abdomen, and you will find that you can still get out a little more, until for a moment quite a pained feeling comes in the chest.

Then inhale *through the nose*, keeping the mouth shut, as long a breath as you can. When you seem unable to inhale any more, raise your elbows to a level at the sides with your shoulders, and work them gently down like a pair of wings, still trying to draw in air, when you will find you can manage to breathe in just a little more. Hold breath not more than a second, and then exhale *through the mouth*, and completely exhaust as before by drawing in the abdomen.

Quality not Quantity.

At first three breaths such as this, deliberately drawn, will suffice, adding an extra breath each day until six are inhaled every morning.

During the course of the day at odd moments, when out of doors, such a breath may now and again be taken.

If about six others during the rest of the day are thus inhaled, making twelve in all, it will be quite sufficient.

The Punching Ball

How this improves the lung capacity can only be understood by one who has put it to the test for six months.

Other Breathing Exercises.

Almost any movements made with the lungs well filled, and held so for a moment, are useful.

Fill lungs, and punch with each arm, holding breath.

Fill lungs, and raise hands from side of hips to full extent above head.

Fill lungs and rotate the trunk from the hips, bending over first to the right side and then to the left.

Bend forward until tips of fingers touch the toes, legs being held straight, expelling air *through the mouth*.

Raise body until arms are straight above head, inhaling *through the nose*. Repeat this three or four times.

The Punching Ball.

The boxer's stock "chest exerciser" is the punching ball, and a very fine thing for the purpose it is, for it not only does wonders for the wind, but teaches quickness of hand and eye at the same time.

Punching balls are of many sorts, but may be divided for all practical purposes into two classes :—

(1) Those that require a wall or platform to play against.

(2) Those which do not.

The "Grasshopper"

The "Grasshopper."

For practice at home, one which will not require a
wall or platform is most useful, such as the "Grass-

THE "GRASSHOPPER."

hopper," an illustration of which I give. These
are so arranged that the height of the ball itself can
be adjusted to suit the height of the user. The top
of the ball should be just above shoulder height.

83

The Army Type

The Army Type.

For gymnasium use, or wherever a wall or platform can be had, the "Army" type is very much

THE "ARMY" PUNCHING BALL.

more to be recommended. It is quicker, more sensitive to the blow, freer in its swing and return, and in
every way better practice, but unsuited for a private

house that is not very substantial, as it throws a lot of strain on the ceiling and wall where it is fixed.

Captain Edgworth-Johnstone holds that no other than the free swinging ball should be used, urging that the "Grasshopper" pattern encourages habits of "flipping." There is something in this, and if the fixed pattern is used, practice should be also obtained whenever possible on the "free" type.

The Platform.

The platform necessary consists of boards of wood joined together to the size of from 4 ft. 6 in. to 6 ft. square, and fastened to the ceiling. From the centre of this the ball is swung. As will be seen in the illustration, the strap adjusted allows the ball to be raised or lowered to suit any height.

There are other punching balls such as the "Moline," which has its own circular hollow gallery in place of the flat platform, but these whilst very excellent are all more or less cumbersome, and unsuited to an amateur's home requirements. This objection, however, is obviated in Messrs. Spalding's Special Platform No. 2. It is light, substantial, and quickly set up.

I have patented a platform which can be fitted on the ground vertically or overhead on a cross-piece held up by four posts, and which I have found in my own experience to do away with the disadvantages mentioned above.

The Medicine Bag

A Home-Made Punching Ball.

Hang either a Rugby or Association football, the latter for preference, from the ceiling with a cord, and it will serve the purpose well.

Some Hints.

The ball may be punched with the naked hands. Some gloves not unlike a housemaid's are sold for the purpose, but I prefer to use actual boxing gloves or an old pair of kid gloves.

Always strike out straight strong hits, and take a rest directly you hit slack.

You can arrange a regular fight with your punching ball—rounds, rests, and all to time, just as if fighting a competitor, and you will find that for a long while all your skill will be required to keep your inanimate opponent from landing!

The Medicine Bag.

This is a small bag full of sand or grain which is thrown alternately with each hand, but not in the ordinary way.

Stand as though boxing, and let each hand throw the bag from its own position, just as if it would have to land a blow were a competitor in front.

Up Stairs and Down.

Running up and down steps is most excellent work for the wind. If it can be done out of doors, as for instance up and down the stairs of a high open grand-stand, so much the better.

Study Variety of Exercise

Runners—sprinters in particular—all take this form of exercise. It strengthens and quickens a man on his legs at the same time.

Sprinting.

One or two sharp bursts of sprinting, for anything from 40 to 200 yards in the course of the day, prepare the lungs to cope with the sudden sharp exertion which boxing always calls upon them to meet.

Skipping.

Skipping is very fine wind exercise. Cyclists in particular favour skipping, but it is equally good as a lung exercise for any branch of sport. It also is good leg muscle work.

About 400 to 1000 skips without stopping at a good pace will puff any but the soundest of wind and limb.

Jumping.

Both long jumping and high jumping put sudden strong efforts on to the lungs, and hence help in their extension and development.

Study Variety of Exercise.

Before leaving this branch of our subject, let me impress the benefit of variety of exercise. One day one thing the next another, is the best plan, and above all never neglect your wind work.

CHAPTER XIV

Training for Boxing

*The best hours—The food question—Breakfast—Dinner
—Tea—Between meals—What to drink—Drink for
abstainers — Moderate sleep — Smoking —Walking—
Running and other exercises—Increase or reduction of
weight—Flannel-wear—Massage.*

The Best Hours.

THERE used to be a widely accepted notion that the
first essential in training, no matter for what sport or
exercise, was early rising. Men used to be hounded
out of bed by their trainers at the most unearthly
hours, and compelled to take sharp running or walking
exercise before breakfast. In training for boxing, at
any rate, opinions on this have greatly changed, but
I notice that. Mr. Allanson-Winn thinks that "early
morning rising and running before breakfast is much
to be commended in many cases," though he em-
phasises the fact that "whenever they harass or worry
they should not be countenanced."

For my own part I do not believe in them. If a
man is down in good time for breakfast, I do not
think the conscience of his trainer need be disturbed.

Perhaps more important than any other point is
that of regularity. The hours may be easy, but they
must be regular.

The Food Question

The Food Question.

The meal times of the ordinary man of business are, curiously enough, the most suitable for the boxer. They differ, however, in one particular. The late dinner is absolutely forbidden.

After rising at about 7.30, a man should find his breakfast ready for him between 8 and half-past. One o'clock finds him sitting down to midday dinner, and by half-past six he has finished his tea.

In recommending a diet I cannot do better than quote the advice of Mr. Harry Andrews,[1] with whose opinion I am in the most cordial agreement.

Mr. Andrews says:—

"FOR BREAKFAST.—A couple of new-laid eggs and toast, followed by a little cress or marmalade, or both; or half a pound of fresh fish and toast, cress or marmalade, or both. A steak or a chop may sometimes take the place of the eggs or fish.

"I disallow bacon and butter, only occasionally permitting just a very little butter to a man who may particularly fancy it.

"FOR DINNER.—Roast beef, mutton, boiled mutton, poultry, game, milk puddings, and stewed fruits, plenty of green vegetables. As great a variety of food as possible from day to day is advisable. I bar pork, rabbit, hare, venison (this is apt to upset the inside), boiled beef and potatoes. No suet puddings or pastry. Shell fish are also taboo, as are all kinds of cheese.

"FOR TEA.—Consists of eggs, fish or poultry, toast

[1] "Training." By Harry Andrews. (C. A. Pearson, Ltd. 1s.)

What to Drink

or crust of bread; the crust should always be toasted and the crust eaten stale, not new. Watercress is allowed, but very little, if any, butter.

"As a general rule, I think it best to let each one regulate the quantities for himself. I find that in the long run they generally level off to about the amounts stated above.

"BETWEEN MEALS.—A biscuit or two, or an apple after the morning exercise, and a biscuit also about nine o'clock in the evening, in addition to the above meals, complete the solid side of the food question."

I would only add to this the use of a little Oxo at meal times. I find it useful as a strength giver, and prefer it to the other essences, as it contains a greater proportion of nourishing matter.

What to Drink.

The drink allowance must naturally be different for the two classes of men who go into training, the teetotallers and the moderate drinkers.

It is no more foolish to tell an abstainer that because he is going into training he must take an alcoholic stimulant, than it is to tell a man accustomed to take a little with his meals that he must not touch a glass of beer. Sudden change must at all costs be avoided.

Those who are moderate takers of alcohol should drink a little weak coffee or tea at breakfast, taking half a pint of old ale or light Burton after the morning exercise. At dinner another half pint is allowed. At teatime he may have a couple of cups of tea. All coffee or tea drunk during training must be weak.

Moderate Sleep

Later on in the evening I have no objection to his drinking another half pint of ale.

A very little champagne has sometimes a useful effect in freshening up an overtrained man, but if given it must be taken instead of the morning half pint of beer; but as a rule some beef-tea in the form of Oxo, the Liebig Company's fluid beef, for two or three days will give the necessary " tone."

Drink for Abstainers.

Abstainers may drink about half a pint of weak tea, coffee, or chocolate, at breakfast, and either water or milk and soda, or better still, a glass of Oxo mixed in hot water, but allowed to become quite cold before it is taken, after morning exercise if they need it. At dinner, in place of the moderate drinker's half pint of ale they may take the same quantity of water or milk and soda or Oxo. The usual two cups of tea are allowed at that meal, and later in the evening a glass of soda and milk.

Moderate Sleep.

Don't take too much sleep. The ordinary business man gets to bed about eleven. Do you do the same. You will be able to get about eight hours sleep and you will need no more. The man who spends a longer time in bed has a tendency towards lassitude very hard to overcome.

Smoking.

I always begin by saying, " Don't smoke." But if the man to be trained is a confirmed smoker I never attempt to deprive him of the pipes after meals, which have become so much a part of his constitution that any deprivation of them is a real hardship. Training never imposes severe hardships, a rule quite worth remembering.

But if you are a non-smoker to begin with, you will undoubtedly have an advantage over the smoker. Very few smokers excel in athletics of any kind. So that if you are only in the early stages of the habit, and can give it up without serious inconvenience, I should most strongly urge you to do so.

In any case, do what you can to reduce the quantity of tobacco you consume. Every ounce you can give up is an ounce on the right side.

Walking.

No exercise is more beneficial to the boxer in training than pedestrianism. I always recommend its wide use. It is almost impossible to walk too much. In walking you use nearly every muscle you possess, and so are doing the work that hours of gymnastic exercise cannot perform. While walking be very careful to finish each breath you take. You breathe in and you breathe out. Let each action be as full as possible.

Running and other Exercises.

Running is considered in the earlier chapter on Wind. In the same chapter will be found various other useful exercises.

Massage

Increase or Reduction of Weight.

In the majority of cases weight is to be got rid of. In a few, however, it is desirable to give a lean man a little extra flesh.

If you wish to lose flesh you must reduce your allowance of liquid food. Starving is to deprecated, though it is always well to come hungry to meals. "Always leave off with an appetite," said an old man of my acquaintance, "and you will always begin with one."

Flannel-wear.

Take exercise in flannels. Sweating will result, and after work a rub down with a hard bath towel is of the utmost value.

It is not at all advisable to take off too much weight. Weakness is the inevitable end of such a course. If you find that you have overdone it, or are too thin, a slight increase in liquid diet will put things right.

Massage.

Massage has been introduced by the Americans as a regular part of training. Their success is great. It removes superfluous fat in the best possible way, and is a fine corrective for stiff muscles.

It is best to get someone else to do the massaging, though if needs be it can always be done at home. Mr. Harry Andrews the famous trainer gives most explicit directions for this operation :—[1]

"Commence by rubbing the chest with one hand and the back with the other, with an upward circular

[1] " Training " By Harry Andrews. (C. A. Pearson Ltd. 1s.)

Massage

motion. Whilst the right hand rubs the left side of the chest, the left hand rubs the right shoulder-blade, and *vice versâ*. In these positions of the arms one can work all over the body, back and front, from the neck down to the top of the thighs. Do not miss a spot. Rub softly and briskly. Between the rubbing catch hold of pieces of flesh between the first finger and thumb, and lightly squeeze them. It is this pinching which is the principal part of my system. Great care must be exercised not to cause bruises.

"This pinching also gets rid of the bad flesh, softens the muscle, and allows it to develop just as it should. Let each hand run over in like fashion the opposite arm, giving the biceps a specially lively pinching. Next pinch the muscles quickly all over the thighs, back and front from the knees to the groin. One hand can take each thigh, and then work from the calves downwards to the ankles and all over the feet.

"To obtain the full benefit, the subject should during massage relax each muscle which is being touched, and in this lies the advantage of having someone to do it for you, as it is much easier to relax your muscles when lying inactive than when you yourself are doing the work, for this in itself is a fairly tiring form of exercise. . . ."

For boxing special attention to the arm and chest muscles is needed. A fine supple muscular development all over the front of chest and stomach is an invaluable equipment of the boxer.

CHAPTER XV

Rules of Boxing

Definition of amateur—Rules of the Amateur Boxing Association—" Sporting Life" revised Queensberry rules—Contests for endurance.

Definition of Amateur.

" An amateur is one who has never competed with or against a professional for any prize, and who has never taught, pursued, or assisted in the practice of athletic exercises as a means of obtaining a livelihood."

Rules of the Amateur Boxing Association.

1. In all competitions the ring shall be roped, and of not less than 12 ft. or more than 24 ft. square.

2. Competitors to box in light boots or shoes (without spikes), or in socks, with knickerbockers, breeches, or trousers, and sleeved jerseys.

3. Weights to be:—Feather, not exceeding 9 st.; light, not exceeding 10 st.; middle, not exceeding 11 st. 4 lb.; heavy, any weight. Competitors to weigh on the day of competition in boxing costume without gloves.

4. In all open competitions the result shall be decided by two judges with a referee. A timekeeper shall be appointed.

5. In all open competitions the number of rounds to

Rules of Boxing Association

be contested shall be three. The duration of the first two rounds shall be three minutes, and of the final round four minutes, and the interval between each round shall be one minute.

6. In all competitions any competitor failing to come up when time is called shall lose the bout.

7. Where a competitor draws a bye, such competitor shall be bound to spar such bye for the specified time, and with such opponent as the judges of such competition may approve.

8. Each competitor shall be entitled to the assistance of one second only, and no advice or coaching shall be given to any competitor by his second, or by any other person, during the progress of any round.

9. The manner of judging shall be as follows: The two judges and the referee shall be stationed apart. At the end of each bout each judge shall notify the name of the competitor who, in his opinion, has won, and shall hand the same to an official appointed for the purpose.

In the cases where the judges agree, such official shall announce the name of the winner; but in cases where the judges disagree, such official shall so inform the referee, who shall thereupon himself decide.

10. The referee shall have power to give his casting vote when the judges disagree, or to stop a round in the event of either man being knocked down; the stopping of either of the first two rounds shall not disqualifiy any competitor from competing in the final round. And he can order a further round limited to two minutes, in the event of the judges disagreeing.

Revised Queensberry Rules

11. The decision of the judges or referee, as the case may be, shall be final and without appeal.

12. In all competitions the decision shall be given in favour of the competitor who displays the best style, and obtains the greatest number of points. The points shall be:—for " Attack," direct clean hits with the knuckles of either hand on any part of the front or sides of the head or body above the belt; " Defence," guarding, slipping, ducking, counter-hitting, or getting away. Where points are otherwise equal, consideration to be given to the man who does most of the leading off.

13. The referee may, after cautioning the offender, disqualify a competitor who is boxing unfairly by flicking or hitting with the open glove, by hitting with the inside or butt of the hand, the wrist or elbow, or wrestling or roughing at the ropes.

14. In the event of any question arising not provided for in these rules, the judges and referee have full power to decide such question or interpretation of rule.

" Sporting Life " Revised Queensberry Rules.

1. The ring shall be roped, and 24 ft. square.

2. Competitors to box in light boots or shoes (without spikes), or in socks, with knickerbockers, breeches, or trousers, and wear jerseys.

3. The result shall be decided by two judges, with a referee, or by a referee only.

4. The number of rounds to be contested shall be three. The duration of the first two rounds shall be

Contests for Endurance

3 min., and of the final round 4 min., and the interval between each round shall be 1 min.

5. Any competitor failing to come up when "Time" is called shall lose the bout.

6. Where a competitor draws a bye, he shall be bound to spar such bye for the specified time, and with such opponent as the judges or referee may approve.

7. Each competitor shall be entitled to the assistance of one attendant only, and no advice or coaching shall be given to any competitor by his second, or by any other person, during the progress of any round.

8. The referee shall have power to give his casting vote when the judges disagree, or to stop the contest in either the second or third round in the event of it being very one-sided; and he can further order a fourth round, limited to two minutes, in the event of the judges disagreeing.

9. That the decision of the judges or referee, as the case may be, shall be final and without appeal.

10. The referee may, after cautioning the offender, disqualify a competitor who is boxing unfairly by flicking or hitting with the open glove, by hitting with the inside or butt of the hand, the wrist or elbow, or by wrestling or roughing at the ropes.

11. In the event of any questions arising not provided for in these rules, the referee to have the full power to decide such question, and his decision to be final.

Contests for Endurance.

To be a fair stand-up boxing match, in a 24 ft. ring, or as near that size as practicable; no wrestling,

Contests for Endurance

hugging, or hanging on allowed. Should a clinch occur, the men to break away immediately, and neither man must deliver a blow without having both hands free. The rounds to be of three (or two) minutes' duration, as may be agreed upon beforehand, with one minute time between each round. If either man fall through weakness or otherwise he must get up unassisted; his opponent meanwhile must not stand over him, but step back out of distance. So soon, however, as the fallen man is on his legs again, his opponent can advance to the attack and continue the onslaught until the round is ended. Should the man fail to rise within ten seconds, the referee to declare his opponent the winner. No seconds or any other person to be allowed in the ring during the rounds. Should the contest be stopped by any unavoidable interference, the referee to name time and place for finishing the contest as soon as possible; the match must be fought to a finish, unless the backers of both men agree to draw the stakes. The gloves to be fair-sized boxing gloves of the best quality, and new; these on no account to be tampered with by the seconds or any one else. Should a glove burst or come off, it must be replaced to the referee's satisfaction. A man on one knee is considered down, and if struck in this position is entitled to the stakes. No shoes or boots with sprigs allowed. The referee has power, in the event of a man being weak and hopelessly beaten, to stop the contest and declare his opponent the winner.

CHAPTER XVI

Boxing   Records

*The history of boxing—Classical boxing bouts—The English
prize-ring—Champions from 1719 to present day—
Amateur champions since 1888—Longest fights—
Shortest fights.*

The History of Boxing.

So long almost as man has existed boxing in one
form or another has had a place amongst his sports.

How the writer's blood tingled and thrilled in his
schooldays at reading of the Homeric and Virgilian
heroes whose cæstus' whacks resounded for fully a
mile, or whose blow crunched bone and flesh together
with dull thud.   And yet the author of the Badminton volume on Boxing sententiously informs us that
"It may be an unpleasant surprise to some of the
great admirers of Boxing to hear that the antiquity
of the art is incapable of being proved, or even
seriously maintained."

Classical Boxing Bouts.

If the fight between Epeus and Eurycles was not
"boxing," the description of its finish sounds as much
like that of a knock-out in the modern ring as well
may be.   Homer concludes: "The divine Epeus,
"landing" upon his adversary, gives him a buffet

on the cheek that makes him drop. He falls; his friends surrounding him carry him away insensible, his legs hanging powerless, his head drooping on his shoulder." A very vigorous style of boxing this appears to have been!

Virgil in his fifth *Æneid* has given an equally vivid description of a boxing match between the veteran Entellus and the younger champion Dares :—

> "The combatants on tiptoe undismayed,
> Their arms uplift in air, their heads withdraw
> Back from the blows, and mingling hand with hand,
> Provoke the conflict.
>
>   .   .   .   .   .
>
> Full many a wound they menace, many a blow
> Hard on the hollow ribs and chest resounds ;
> The hand now hovers about ears and brow,
> Now on the cheek with heavy crash it falls.
> Dares, like one who doth his batteries ply
> Against a city or a mountain fort,
> Tries this approach and that, on every side
> The assault renews and varies, but in vain.
> Entellus him with lifted arm essays
> To strike, but all alert the coming blow
> He saw, and with a sudden spring eludes:
> The blow was spent in air, and after it
> Entellus to the ground with all his weight
> Heavily falls ; but to the fight returns
> And Dares over all the field he drives,
> Dealing his blows with right hand and with left,
> Impetuous, irresistible."

The English Prize-Ring.

In England our record of Champion Prize-fighters goes back to about the year 1719, and I give a list from that date, for which I am indebted to that

Champions from 1719

excellent compendium of all sorts of sporting and athletic records, issued by the *Sporting Life* at twopence
annually, called the *Sporting Life Companion*.

Champions from 1719 to Present Day.

1719. Figg.
1730. Pipes and Greeting.
1734. George Taylor.
1740. Jack Broughton.
1750. Jack Slack.
1760. Bill Stevens.
1761. George Meggs.
1764. Bill Darts.
1769. Lyons.
1777. Harry Sellers.
1780. Harris.
1785. Jackling, Tom (*alias* Johnson).
1790. Ryan (Big Ben).
1792. Mendoza.
1795. Jackson (retired).
1803. Jem Belcher.
1805. Pearce (Game Chicken).
1808. Gulley (declined the office).
1809. Tom Cribb (received a belt, not transferable, and cup).
1824. Tom Spring (received four cups and resigned office).
1825. Jem Ward (received a belt, not transferable).
1833. Deaf Burke (claimed the office).
1839. Bendigo (W. Thompson) (beat Deaf Burke, claimed
 championship, and received a belt from Jem
 Ward).
1841. Nick Ward (brother to Jem) beat Caunt, Feb. 2.
 Caunt (beat Nick Ward, and received a belt by
 subscription. The belt was transferable).

1845. Bendigo (beat Caunt, and got the belt).

1849. Tass Parker (beat Con Parker for £100 a-side and the Championship).

1850. Perry (the Tipton Slasher), after his fight with Paddock, claimed the office.

1851. Harry Broome (beat Perry, and succeeded to the office).

1853. Perry again claimed the office, Harry Broome having forfeited £20 to him in a match, and retired from the Ring on August 13.

1857. Tom Sayers (beat Perry for £200 a-side and the new belt).

1860. Tom Sayers retired after his fight with Heenan, leaving the old belt open for competition.

1860. Sam Hurst (the Stalybridge Infant) beat Paddock. Both claimed the office of Champion. The belt handed to Hurst.

1861. Jem Mace (beat Hurst).

1862. Jem Mace beat Tom King (January) for £200 and the belt.

1862. Tom King beat Mace (November) and claimed the belt, which he subsequently gave up, declining again to meet Mace. Mace again claimed the belt.

1865. Joe Wormald beat Marsden, £200 a-side and the belt, both having claimed the Championship. Belt handed to Wormald. Forfeited £120 to Mace, who again claimed.

1866. Jem Mace and Joe Goss (a draw, £200 a-side and the belt).

1867. Joe Wormald received forfeit from E. Baldwin, £200 and the Championship. Baldwin absent at the starting place. Wormald claimed the belt.

1867. Jem Mace and E. Baldwin (a draw, £200 a-side and the Championship. The belt in abeyance).

1868. J. Wormald and E. Baldwin (a draw, £200 a-side and the title, in America).

1869. M'Coole beat T. Allen, in America, for Championship of the World.

1870. Jem Mace beat T. Allen, in America, for Championship of the World.

1872. Jem Mace and J. Coburn fought a draw for £500 a-side and the Championship.

1885. Jem Smith beat Jack Davies for £100 a-side and the Championship of England.

1886. Jem Smith and Alf Greenfield, for £600 and Championship, fought a draw (February 16).

1887. Jake Kilrain and Jem Smith (a draw, £2000 and Championship of the World).

1888. John L. Sullivan and C. Mitchell fought a draw, Chantilly, France (39 rounds, in 3 hours 11 min.).

1889. John L. Sullivan beat Jake Kilrain for £2000 a-side, at Richburg, New Orleans (July 8).

1889. Jem Smith and Frank P. Slavin fought a draw for £500 a-side and Championship of England, Bruges (December 23).

The Amateur Champions since 1888.

BANTAM WEIGHTS (8 st. 4 lb. and under).

1888. H. C. M. Oakman	1896. P. A. Jones
1889. H. Brown	1897. C. T. Lamb
1890. J. J. Rowe	1898. F. K. Herring
1891. E. Moore	1899. A. Avent
1892. F. Godbold	1900. J. Freeman
1893. E. A. Watson	1901. W. Morgan
1894. P. A. Jones	1902. A. J. Miner
1895. P. A. Jones	

Amateur Champions since 1888

FEATHER WEIGHTS (9 st. and under).

1888. J. E. Taylor
1889. T. J. M'Neill
1890. G. F. Belsey
1891. F. Curtis
1892. F. Curtis
1893. T. F. Davidson
1894. R. K. Gunn
1895. R. K. Gunn

1896. R. K. Gunn
1897. N. T. Smith
1898. P. A. Lunn
1899. J. L. Scholes
1900. R. Lee
1901. C. J. Clarke
1902. C. J. Clarke

LIGHT WEIGHTS (10 st. and under).

1888. A. J. Newton
1889. W. Neale
1890. A. J. Newton
1891. E. Dettmer
1892. E. Dettmer
1893. W. Campbell
1894. W. Campbell
1895. A. Randall

1896. A. Vanderhout
1897. A. Vanderhout
1898. H. Marks
1899. H. Brewer
1900. G. W. Humphries
1901. A. Warner
1902. A. Warner

MIDDLE WEIGHTS (11 st. 4 lb. and under).

1888. R. Hair
1889. G. Skyes
1890. J. Hoare
1891. J. Steers
1892. J. Steers
1893. J. Steers
1894. W. Skyes
1895. G. L. Townsend

1896. W. L. Ross
1897. W. Dees
1898. G. L. Townsend
1899. R. C. Warnes
1900. E. Mann
1901. R. C. Warnes
1902. E. Mann

Longest Fights

HEAVY WEIGHTS (any weight).

1888. W. J. King	1895. ⎱ Capt. Edgworth-
1889. A. Bowman	1896. ⎰ Johnstone
1890. J. Steers	1897. G. L. Townsend
1891. Val Barker	1898. G. L. Townsend
1892. J. Steers	1899. T. Parks
1893. J. Steers	1900. W. Dees
1894. Horace King	1901. F. Parks
	1902. F. Parks

Longest Fights.

The length of time which some fights have lasted seems almost incredible to any one who knows how much a sharply contested three-round competition bout will take out of a man, if he puts forth his best and is well matched.

In Australia near Melbourne, during November 1855, James Kelly and Jonathan Smith fought for 6 hours and 15 minutes.

One hundred and eighty-five rounds in 6 hours and 3 minutes was the duration of one of Mike Maddens' fights in July 17, 1849, at Edenbridge, with Bill Hayes for opponent. The same Mike Maddens the year before had a 5 hour and 45 minute contest (one hundred and forty rounds) with one Jack Grant at Woking.

A glove fight, however, lasted still longer than either of the above. For 7 hours and 19 minutes (one hundred and ten rounds), A. Bowen and J. Burke punched at each other at New Orleans, U.S.A., on April 6, 1893.

Shortest Fights

It seems hard lines on those who had fought so long that neither could claim a win, for the result was a draw.

Shortest Fights.

In sharp contrast to the above are the shortest combats.

At Carbondale, Pa, U.S.A., Hearld knocked out Cannon in 30 seconds on May 23, 1886. Once again the gloves hold a record that beats fists, for on March 17, 1897, Dal Hawkins finished his bout with Martin Flaherty at Carson City, Nevada, in the double quick time of 4 seconds. Not much of a contest for the onlookers!

Single-Stick

The Advantages of Single-Stick.

SINGLE-STICK, as a manly sport, is much more than a mere recreation. It is closely akin to sword-play and fencing in its chief characteristics and results, for it very decidedly promotes both bodily and mental culture, calling many muscles into healthful play, and teaching invaluable lessons of patience, alertness, and self-command.

The great charm of all sword-play is that it induces quickness not only of action but of thought, for as our brain is the controlling power, the more sharp-set its functions the better our movements are conceived and carried out.

Its Practical Value.

Another and a very practical advantage, which is gained by those who learn to use a stick with skill and science, is that they thus have ready to hand a simple and effective weapon for self-defence in any real emergency.

The sight is also trained, though not strained as in some sports, for it is of the greatest importance to watch for an opening, and as soon as one is seen to take advantage of it.

Its Early Forms

An Old English Sport.

Single-stick is among the oldest British sports, and on the green of many a country village our fore-fathers used to meet and cut away—it may be in very unscientific form—for wagers redeemable in good nut-brown ale.

Its Early Forms.

In the Badminton Book on Fencing we find a quotation from Mr. Egerton Castle's "Schools and Masters of Fence," which runs thus: "We find it laid down that 'the single-stick or cudgel was, and is, the foil of the back sword.' The author tells us that in England in the sixteenth century the 'waster,' a dummy sword, with a blade rendered harmless by being rounded or transversely set, was the foil of the back sword; and that in the early seventeenth century the name 'waster' was applied to cudgels inserted in sword guards."

Here evidently was the early form of that sub-stitute for an offensive and defensive edged weapon, which has found its latest development in the single-stick of the present day. This may be said to cor-respond, in a very rough and ready fashion, to the modern sabre, just as the "waster," or in later times the form of single-stick, described in the second chapter of "Tom Brown's School Days," corresponded to the sword.

Ancient Cudgels.

Cudgel fighting in the old days was no light matter, and often descended from innocent sport to sheer brutality; and to such mutual mauling as was a

disgrace to humanity. They took their sports and plea-
sures very seriously in those olden days, and victory
for one man meant crushing defeat for his opponent.

We must admit that the fifteenth and sixteenth cen-
turies produced much better men, physically speaking,
than are in existence to-day. Their life was more
strenuous, rougher in every detail, and consequently
their sports were coarser. But out of these question-
able qualities has come much good to successive
generations.

Modern Experience.

To-day in many of our public schools single-stick
practice is recommended for every boy's physical culture. From this point of view the sport is certainly
excellent. Almost every muscle of the body is brought
into play and duly exercised.

Not only are the muscles of the arm thoroughly
involved, but the leg and body muscles also come into
play with nearly every stroke. The inexperienced
will better appreciate this after the first half-hour's
practice. Not only will their arms ache, but their
thighs and abdomens will tell of the calls that have
been made upon them.

I remember that on the day after my first-hour
with the sticks I could hardly walk to school, so stiff
were my lower limbs. This soon wore off, however,
and after a few days' work I could lunge continually
without feeling any ill effects.

Single-stick may become in careless hands a
dangerous sport, but if the proper apparatus is used
no serious injuries can befall the combatants.

Necessary Apparatus

A Serious Word of Advice.

A word of advice which should be printed in largest letters is, NEVER BE TEMPTED INTO PRACTISING WITHOUT THE PROPER PROTECTIVE APPARATUS OVER THE FACE. It is so easy to pick up a stick, and to start cutting and thrusting, and it is so easy to send the point of the stick into an opponent's face, thus causing without intention an injury that may lead to lifelong regret and lifelong misery.

Necessary Apparatus.

The single-stick itself is generally fashioned from a plain ash staff, and is as a rule forty inches in length, and three-quarters of an inch in thickness. The handle or hilt is made of basket-work. The stick runs through two holes in this, and is prevented from slipping out by a cross peg at one end.

The basket must run easily up and down the stick, so that, in the case of a thrust, when the point reaches the opponent's body, the shock will not be too severe.

The Helmet.

In addition to the single-stick, an iron meshed helmet is necessary. This is in reality a mask, covers the face, fits under the chin, and is held firmly in its place by an iron band which passes over the back of the head. Care should be taken that the helmet fits tightly, as the jar caused by a blow with a single-stick is often very keenly felt if this protection is at all loose, for single-stick, unlike the foil, does not give on coming in contact with a rigid body.

The Gauntlet

The Jacket.

Most men when practising with single-stick wear a leathern jacket sufficiently padded to withstand the heavier cuts. This is something like a tight-fitting Eton coat, and should be made of good stout material.

Leg Guards.

The right leg of the single-stick player is perhaps most open to punishment, and in consequence of this many men wear a leathern apron over their leg, whilst others strap on to their thigh a sort of half gauntlet.

The Gauntlet.

It is as well for the amateur to wear a stiff leathern gauntlet, as at first his right wrist and forearm will come in for some very heavy punishment.

It must always be remembered, in taking these precautions, that there is very little real sport where there is no danger. If the fighter is so guarded that he has nothing to fear from the heavy cuts of his opponent, then he will not take sufficient care to guard against these blows. Where every blow that reaches home means physical pain, the wits of the combatants are sharpened, and the corresponding quickness of movement will result.

Another important point is this. If the player is bound up in stiff padded clothing, every movement will either be jerky, or extremely slow. After all a cut from a single-stick is not such a serious matter, and after the first two or three days will hardly be noticed.

The Proper Grip

Keep Your Temper.

Another piece of advice I should like to give to every wielder of the ash is this, be good tempered. Never let your temper run away with you, for invariably the result is increased punishment to yourself. Often when a smart heavy blow comes down on the inside of the leg, or across the ribs, the first thing thought of is how best to pay it back.

After each hit should come immediate recognition or acknowledgment. If the man suffering from the smart of a nasty cut, instead of coming up to the position for acknowledging the stroke—as described later on in this chapter—cuts savagely at his opponent, he will probably find him off his guard and by administering a severe blow will but make matters worse.

In competitions these counter cuts after a hit do not count, and in some cases the man first hit is severely dealt with by the judges. I have seen in a first class competition a man absolutely disqualified for this practice after having once been warned.

It has been impossible in this chapter to go very clearly into the subject, but the instruction given, based on actual experience, will be found sufficient for all practical purposes.

The Proper Grip.

The best way to hold the stick is to close all the fingers round the hilt, and to place the thumb on, or

113   H

Engage !

rather along, the stick. Grasping your weapon in this position, you will find that each stroke can be administered with quick and telling force. The knuckles, meantime, are in the basket, and the base of the thumb is slightly exposed.

On Guard.

When prepared for action the body should be perfectly upright, the legs, together with the right foot, pointing straight to your opponent, and the left foot set square to the other. Hold the basket hilt close into your side, with the point of the stick in the air.

The left hand is kept behind the back, and does not play such an important part as in foil fencing.

Engage !

To "engage" you step forward with the right foot a distance of about two feet, and bend the right knee slightly. The left foot does not move, but the left knee is slightly bent to give ease of action. Do not get too far down, for this would cramp the muscles you really want to bring into a working position.

When "getting down to it" see that the body keeps a fairly upright position, though of course it should not be held too stiffly, for it must work with the right arm to a considerable extent, and on the occasion of a lunge or long cut must get well forward.

The weapon should be held either in the upward guard or else in the downward guard. The former

Which Guard is Best?

is perhaps the best guard to commence with, as the position is not strained, and many amateurs can deliver a quicker attack from this position.

The Upward Guard.

For the upward guard the elbow is dropped close in to the body, and the hand is brought level with the chest. The stick is kept in line with the forearm, and the point should be a little way above the head. The wrist will be slightly turned, so that the basket inclines to the right. Keep the point of your stick well over to your adversary, making with it an angle of about 40°.

Do not get your arm into any fixed position, or tighten up your muscles too rigidly, or you will make the next movement quite a wrench.

The elbow must be kept well inside the basket, and guarded from attack.

The Downward Guard.

The downward guard is the reverse of this. The arm is raised until the hand is almost in front of the face, and the stick points downwards, and towards the enemy. The arm must be kept bent and well out of the way of attack.

Which Guard is Best?

In support of the statement that the upward guard is better than the other, I may quote from Mr. C. Phillips-Wolley's "Broadsword and Single-stick." He says: "Although I have been taught to use the

Army Manual Instructions

hanging guard myself ever since I began to play, I
unhesitatingly say that the upright guard is the better
one, as enabling a player to save time in the attack.
In the hanging guard the knuckles (*i.e.* the edge) are
up and away from the enemy; the wrist must be
turned before the edge can be brought into contact
with his body, and this takes time, however little.

"In the upright guard the knuckles (*i.e.* the edge)
are towards your opponent, the arm is flexed, every
thing is in readiness for the blow. If then, as I believe, the advantages of the two guards, as guards, are
equal, the advantage of the upright guard as a position
to attack from seems to me undeniable."

Army Manual Instructions.

The instructions given in the Army manual of
instruction for the engage and assault are as
follows:—

"*Engage.*—Advance the right foot about sixteen
or eighteen inches straight to the front, and plant it
firmly on the ground, both knees well bent and turned
out, the body erect, left shoulder thrown back, head
kept well up, eyes directed to the front, and . . .
fixed on the opponent's eyes. At the same time
carry the sword straight to the front, its point about
in line with the left eye, the 'forte' or strong part
of the blade covering the right breast, edge to the
front and in line with the knuckles, the back of the
hand up, and about in line with the centre of the top
muscle of the arm; the elbow about six inches from
the body, the blade of the sword a continuation of

A Caution

the forearm, so as to form a direct line from elbow to point. The part of the stick which is in line with the knuckles represents the edge. The stick at all times to be grasped in the same manner as a sword."

Assault.

Make a sharp back-handed cut, and place the back of the sword on the right shoulder, which should be thrown a little back, hand in line with the forehead, elbow under the hand.

This assault is but the preliminary to cut number one. The instructions given run as follows:—"Make a sharp diagonal cut that would enter the left side of the opponent's neck, and if continued pass out through the right breast.

"At the time of delivering the cut advance the right foot sixteen or eighteen inches further to the front, and place it firmly on the ground. The moment the right foot quits the ground to advance, stiffen the left leg up, and brace the knee firmly back, the left foot firm and flat on the ground, body and head erect."

A Caution.

Great care must be exercised when practising this cut, that the step forward is not overdone, for the result of going too far forward with the right foot will be to overbalance the body. In the movement of the right foot care must be taken to see that it does not move out of a straight line.

The Four Cuts

The Left Leg.

The use of the left leg will at first cause the amateur some trouble. Every movement of the right foot must be well followed up by the left leg. If the movement of the feet are not perfectly regulated, nothing but evil will ensue.

To recover from the position resulting from "cut one," the left knee is bent and forced well out; at the same time you must press strongly off the right foot and place it back in the original "engage" position.

The Four Cuts.

There are really only four cuts, which may be called—

1. The right face cut.
2. The left face cut.
3. The left rib cut.
4. The right rib cut.

The famous cuts at the right leg are variations of the rib cut.

The right face cut is executed as follows. From your position on guard lunge out at your opponent's face, and give the cut across from the right side of the neck towards the left breast. In all these cuts plenty of weight must be put behind each stroke, so that even if the correct guard is put up, it may be broken down. We read in ancient history of tremendous blows that have shivered lances, helmets, and armour, and men were no stronger then than now.

Keep a Straight Arm

Cut number three is a lunge from the "engage," and an almost horizontal stroke from right to left; the cut, says the regulations, "being directed between the armpit and the hips on the opponent's left side."

At the end of this stroke the arm should be practically straight. The movement should be a quick one, and should proceed almost entirely from the wrist.

Although it is as well to get back quickly for the next stroke on guard, see that a due amount of work is put into the cut. There is often a tendency just to tap the opponent, which is of little use in serious work.

Cut number four is made on the lunge, and delivered horizontally from left to right at the ribs.

The cuts at the leg are made in an exactly similar manner to the cuts at the ribs, only of course lower down.

Keep a Straight Arm.

The Army regulations contain the following advice: "The instructor must be most careful to impress upon the men the necessity of delivering every cut with a straight arm, and any tendency to wrist cutting (which is impossible with a heavy sword) must be checked at once."

It must of course be remembered that the practice of single-stick among Army men is only a means to an end—the ultimate use of a sword. But if single-stick is to be merely a sport, a good wrist cut may now and again prove very effective.

The Guards

The Thrust.

There is one more mode of dealing punishment, and that is "the thrust." This is delivered straight from the shoulder, and will often be found very effective.

It is as well when thrusting, and sure of your point, to loosen hold of the handle of the stick so that it may run back immediately it touches your opponent's body. With the handle held stiffly it is quite an easy matter to deal a severe wound to your friend the enemy, and this is what is hardly desired when "playing."

The Guards.

Having considered the four cuts, let us now study the various guards for protection from an onset.

The guard for cut number one (at the right face) is a rather high guard upwards. The elbow should be dropped, and the stick, with the edge to the right, should be carried over in that direction. The neck and face must be well guarded. The elbow is a few inches further in than the hand, and the stick points outwards, and slightly towards the opponent.

The guard for the second cut is described as follows in the regulations: "Drop the point until about in line with the left breast and throw the hand smartly over to the left a few inches above and in advance of the head. Should the assailant's cut be delivered perpendicularly, keep the hand over to the right so as to bring the 'forte' of the sword above the head and the point inclined to the left front."

The Recovery

The third guard is managed by dropping the point of the stick and raising the elbow and hand up to a level with the shoulder. The arm should be straightened out, and the sword dipped to a point level with the face.

The fourth guard is executed by raising the hand over to a position in front of the left breast nipple, the stick pointing downwards. The top part of the sword or "forte" will guard the ribs; the elbow is kept well down, and inside the guard.

These four guards should be practised as often as is possible against a quick opponent. The cuts at the leg are parried or guarded by low down variations of guards three and four.

The Recovery.

I have got to mention the matter of recovery. We have already seen that care must be taken not to let the body overbalance when lunging forward. The value of this advice will be appreciated by the novice when he endeavours to recover from an injudicious lunge.

When dealing a cut the whole weight of the body practically goes on to the right foot. In the recovery this is shifted back to the left foot, and then, by pressing with the right foot on the floor, the spring back to the original position can be effected.

Feinting.

There is more skill required in successful feinting than one would at first imagine. Every feint impro-

Acknowledging a Blow

perly executed means loss of time, and a splendid opportunity for your opponent to come in with a smashing cut.

When making a feint one should be careful to see that it is going to lead to something advantageous. The object of this ruse is simply to throw your opponent off his guard, so as to secure an opening in another quarter.

It is impossible to describe a feint further than to say that it is an ordinary cut never intended to be delivered. A man may apparently start to lunge at your head, and while you are raising your guard a horrible crash comes down on the inside of your right leg. The best feints are those in which you draw a man on to believe he will get a cut home, whilst when the actual cut comes, it is parried, and you effect the blow you have really been scheming for.

Acknowledging a Blow.

Every blow received must be acknowledged before play is proceeded with. The mode of acknowledgment is as follows: Immediately you receive the cut draw the feet close together, and stand with body erect, sword upright, and basket just underneath the chin. The edge of your sword will be towards your opponent. Do not waste any time over this business; just spring up, raise the sword, and then get down to business again.

A Foul.

Any hit given in return for a hit received is considered a foul. In competitions each foul takes so many marks off the score. All such fouls should be very heavily dealt with, as they are, generally, the result of bad temper. Now and again, however, a foul cannot be avoided, as on the occasion of two almost simultaneous hits.

Army Rules.

The following Rules are given in the Army Book :—

I. The adversaries should fall in at "the slope," just beyond striking distance, and on the command "Attack" should come to the "Engage," and each make a short step to the front.

II. Cuts only count that are given with the edge of the sword.

III. When both adversaries attack at the same time and in the same position and both hits are "on," neither of the hits counts.

IV. If both attack, and are "on" together, but only one lunges, the point or "cut" of the one who lunges counts.

V. A second attack on the one lunge may be made, but if at the time of the second attack a "return" be made, and both are "on," the "return" only counts.

VI. "Cuts" and "points" are fair all over the body, head, arms, or legs.

VII. Military matters only.

VIII. In competitions, if men frequently counter each other, the judges may, after due warning, (1) disqualify both competitors, or (2) order one to guard and the other to defend, and after a few hits change the order ; and then the man who shows the better knowledge of the two should be declared the winner.

Keep Calm

A "return" is an attack made after a successful guard or parry, and it should be impressed upon the men that a return cannot be made too quickly.

Masks and jackets should always be worn at loose play.

Vary your Opponents.

It is not advisable for the amateur to get into the habit of always playing with the same man. The opponents should be varied. This advice will appeal to all who are going in for a competition, for no two men do the same thing alike, and certainly no two men fence or exercise with single-sticks in a similar manner.

Keep Calm.

Above all things and at all times let no one lose his head when severely punished. Recklessness is bound to result, and further punishment will follow. It is best to speak as little as possible. Mr. Wolley's words on this point are very valuable. He says: "Don't make any remarks either in a competition (this, of course, is worst of all) or in an ordinary bout. Don't argue, except with sticks. Remember that the beau-ideal swordsman is one who fights hard with 'silent lips and striking hand.'"

Printed by BALLANTYNE, HANSON & Co.
Edinburgh & London

ATHLETIC SPORTS.

Camping Out

For Boy Scouts and others
The Whole Art of Living under Canvas.

By VICTOR BRIDGES.

With an Introduction by
LIEUT.-GENERAL BADEN-POWELL.

Price 1s., *post free* **1s. 2d.**

Limp cloth.

Swimming

BY
MONTAGUE A. HOLBEIN,
The well-known Channel Swimmer.
With Illustrations.
Cloth, **Price 1s.**, *post free* **1s. 2d.**

The Contents include :—

Floating—Breast Stroke — Swimming on the Back —Sea Swimming —The Overhand Stroke — Treading Water — Under Water Swimming — Swimming Like a Dog—Plunging and Diving—Training—Life Saving, etc.

Rowing and Sculling

By W. G. EAST,
Ex-Champion Sculler of the Thames, and Bargemaster to H.M. King Edward VII.

Cloth, **Price 1s.**, *post free* **1s. 2d.**

A thoroughly practical handbook by an expert, with 20 illustrations showing correct and incorrect positions.

Practical Fishing

FOR THE SO-CALLED COARSE FISHES.

A Complete Treatise on Float-Fishing & Legering, Spinning, Trolling, and Live Baiting on River, Lake and Stream.

BY
J. W. MARTIN,
"The Trent Otter."
Author of "Float-Fishing in the Nottingham Style," "Barbel and Chub Fishing," etc., etc.

Illustrated.

Price 1s., *post free* **1s. 2d.**

Cricket

EDITED BY
GILBERT L. JESSOP.
Cloth, **Price 1s.**, *post free* **1s. 2d.**
The Contents include Contributions by
K. S. RANJITSINHJI, C. B. FRY, G. L. JESSOP, C. L. TOWNSEND, AND GEO. BRANN.

Boxing

With a Selection on Singlestick.

BY
A. J. NEWTON,
Lightweight Amateur Champion,
1888 *and* 1890.
With
20 Illustrations.
Cloth,
Price 1s.,
post free
1s. 2d.

The above volumes may be had of all Booksellers, or post free from the Publishers,
C. Arthur Pearson, Ltd., 17–18 Henrietta Street, London, W.C.